Love in a Time of Crisis and Pandemic

Messages for Our Children and Grandchildren

Bruce G. Epperly

Energion Publications
Gonzalez, Florida
2021

ISBN: 978-1-63199-683-2
eISBN: 978-1-63199-684-9

Energion Publications
PO Box 841
Gonzalez, FL 32560

https://energion.com
pubs@energion.com

TABLE OF CONTENTS

Acknowledgments

Dedicated to my grandsons Jack and James
and to children, parents, and grandparents everywhere
with the hope that love and joy abound in every household,
on city streets, and country thoroughfares across our planet.
May they live in a land where justice serves everyone,
freedom rings for every child,
 leaders are compassionate to the vulnerable,
 and faith and science are companions in truth-seeking.
May the adults in their lives bring beauty to the earth
 as they look seven generations ahead
 with every important decision.
Let there be peace on earth and let it begin with us.

CHAPTER ONE

THE STILL SMALL VOICE

"Go out and stand on the mountain before GOD, for GOD is about to pass by." Now there was a great wind, so strong that it was splitting mountains and breaking rocks in pieces before God, but GOD was not in the wind; and after the wind an earthquake, but GOD was not in the earthquake, and after the earthquake a fire, but GOD was not in the fire, and after the fire a sound of sheer silence. When Elijah heard it, he wrapped his face in his mantle and went out and stood at the entrance of the cave. Then there came a voice to him that said, "What are you doing here, Elijah?" (I Kings 19:11–13, AP)

There is a great storm out there and we are all anxious. It's not a thunderstorm or blizzard. It's not a tidal wave or hurricane. It's a tiny virus that has turned your world upside down. The Coronavirus has closed your school and shuttered our church. These days, we can't go to our favorite pizza spot and have to wear masks to play on the beach. We can't go to dinner and a movie, because all the theatres are closed and our favorite restaurants are doing curbside carry-out, and we're missing playing with friends and going to see our favorite teams play. Although we are phasing in, moving toward a "new normal," school, sports, and church will be different than before. We will have to be careful about what we once did without thinking — hugging, bumping each other, playing around, or spending time with your cousins. Even at school, you will have to wear masks and practice safe distancing. It's even possible that kids in your class will test positive for the virus and you'll have to study online once more.

Zoom was ok for classes and playdates this Spring and Summer, and you can play with Legos and action figures with friends on Zoom. You can meet with your classmates on Zoom. But it's not the same as being together face to face. It's not the same as kicking a goal or shooting a basket or giving each other high fives after winning a game without worrying about catching the virus. This Fall, you didn't go trick or treating in the neighborhood and we didn't sing carols and light candles in person at church on Christmas Eve. Less than a year ago, we never heard the word COVID-19 and now it's at the heart of everything we do!

It's tough to be a kid these days, and just as tough to be an adult when your children and grandchildren are feeling anxious and miss doing what kids are supposed to do.

I'm a writer. Writing helps me think things through and to share what's most important to me. When I write, I hear that still small voice of wisdom that helps me find my way and point out a pathway to others. For me, writing is a way of praying which helps me to understand the world and where we fit in, especially in times like these. I write to share my feelings and thoughts and the wisdom I receive. I write to help others make sense of the world and find guideposts for their own lives.

These days I write when I feel inspired. On May 3, 2020, as I was walking on the beach near our home on Cape Cod, Massachusetts, I was thinking of the two of you and our life together, and something remarkable happened. I heard a whisper, a quiet voice, telling me to share something of this time with you.

Remembering is important. When we remember, we recall what it was like to be alive as the stories say, "once upon a time." Looking at our unique place and time, we find perspective and a vantage point to discover new things, and recall that even in difficult times, there is beauty as well as pain and love as well as worry.

I hope the storm of pandemic is over soon and the theme of this book will be in the past, but this storm, COVID-19, will shape your lives forever. You may even mark time by it — BP and AP, "before pandemic" and "after pandemic." It is important to make sense of it right now, to find ways to be happy, enjoy your lives, and grow in mind, body, and spirit. It's important to be safe but also to have fun and reach out to others. It is important to grow in love and faith.

This is not lost time in which nothing happens. This is the time of your life and you need to live it fully each day. If we take each day as an opportunity for growth, we'll always remember this time and the values we learned during this time of pandemic and protest. Hard times can be good times when we focus on what's really important — love, learning, and living each day as an unrepeatable and holy adventure.

This also a memory book so that many years from now, when you are adults with children of your own, you will remember what the world was like through my eyes — and the eyes of the adults who loved you — during this troubled time. A difficult time which was also a beautiful time. A time of love and learning. We were stressed and afraid, but we also played and laughed. During the time of pandemic, we got to share our love for each other in new ways. We saw more of each other and I hope that lasts. Hopefully, you will carry the closeness with your family during this time your whole lives.

I am sharing what was important to me during a time in which you spent almost every day at our home, doing schoolwork, playing sports and Legos, going to the seashore. and imagining alternative worlds where you are superheroes and adventurers. And finally preparing to go back to school and facing the challenges of school, sports, and everyday life in a time of pandemic.

I am a magus by calling and profession. A magus (a member of the magi) is someone who looks at the movements of the stars above and the spirit within and tries to bring the wisdom of the One who Creates the stars and our spirits to our everyday lives. I am a humble member of the line of the three wise men who visited the baby Jesus. I am sure that there were and still are plenty of wise women as well! Some call them wizards and Jedi — like Gandalf, Albus Dumbledore, and Obi Wan Kenobi and Yoda. I come from a tradition of wise women and men, mystics and healers, prophets and shaman, philosophers and teachers who seek to teach truth that grows our souls and shines a light that helps us get through the darkness. As followers of God's light, the light of the world, we are healers, truth-tellers, and people who try to see clearly what's happening around us and discern what's beneath the surface of life. We look for the news beneath the news. The messages of the stars and the messages of this moment of history.

Magi are the spiritual teachers of children, who put them on our knees and bless them, as Jesus did. We raise up new generations of magi as Jesus did when he shared spiritual mysteries with Mary of Magdala and inspired the boy with five loaves to feed five thousand hungry people to show how something as small as a few morsels of food can change the world. A child can do great things. As Gandalf brought out the large spirits of Frodo and Bilbo. As Dumbledore guided Harry Potter, Ron Weasley, and Hermione Granger in their battle against the nameless evil. As Yoda and Obi mentored Luke, helping him realize his identity as a Jedi, a keeper of the light.

You too are in battle mode, like Rae and Luke and Harry, Hermione, and Ron, and you will need to summon up the light and love within you to bring beauty and love to this dark time. It is my vocation to help you be light-bearers whose inner light charts your path through this chaos and gives light for others.

Magi use words and prayers, chants and energy, and mind and heart, but most of all they use love to bring forth power that heals. We are living through a storm like none other, and as powerless as we feel, we have an inner power that will get us through. We can't see what's ahead of us, but it will pass and we will still be standing. Even in the storm you have one freedom — the power to be your best self, to find courage despite your fear, and to let the light within you guide your way. Even in the storm, you are safe because you are surrounded by Love.

There is danger in the storm. That's why we're being careful, sheltering in our homes, wearing masks, washing our hands and keeping a safe physical distance from people we don't know. Even when we go back to school, we will have to be alert and careful. In times of danger, we need words and words have power. And so, I will give you words to help guide you to the other side.

So, boys — and every child who reads this — as you begin your journey of life, I give you my wisdom — the wisdom of the magi — to face whatever comes with courage, love, and hope. I will share the values I hold dear — and experiences that I've had during this time of pandemic which has turned our lives upside down. And, even when you're afraid — and every magus is afraid when they face the powers of evil — you can say a prayer and summon the courage of your higher self, the better angels of God that live in each of us, and go forward as a light bearers in the darkness.

Words matter. Holy words matter. They give us strength and heal our wounds. Songs you can sing. Chants and runes you can repeat. They come from the Holy One and bring forth the Holy with vibrations that change our cells and our souls. Words help us face the storm, knowing that in the darkest night the eye begins to see. And, so I will share words to be guiding lights in the storm and reminders of what it was like once upon a time when a virus swept the land. Life is more than words, but let these words be lanterns for the heroic journey that lies ahead for you and reminders that this is a time for love.

A Simple Prayer

Every heroic journey inspires prayers. Our prayers are a heartfelt opening to Wisdom and Power Beyond Yourself and your desire to be part of a bigger story of saving the earth and bringing love to those around you.

The story is told of St. Patrick being pursued by the knights of an Irish chieftain. There was a bounty for capturing or killing him. On one of his journeys, Patrick heard the thundering sounds of horses behind him. He knew this meant only one thing. The chieftain's soldiers had discovered him and would likely capture him. According to legend, Patrick stepped in the woods beside the road and said a prayer of protection. When the soldiers rode by, all they saw was a deer bounding across the road.

Patrick's prayer of protection is known as the Breastplate or the Deer Cry. I can imagine the saint performing an ancient Celt-

ic practice called the *caim* or encircling and then saying a special
prayer that people still use today:

> Christ shield me today
> Against wounding.
> Christ with me, Christ before me, Christ behind me,
> Christ in me, Christ beneath me, Christ above me,
> Christ on my right, Christ on my left,
> Christ when I lie down, Christ when I sit down,
> Christ in the heart of everyone who thinks of me,
> Christ in the mouth of everyone who speaks of me,
> Christ in the eye that sees me,
> Christ in the ear that hears me.

For Patrick and me, Christ is the power of love that includes
and empowers everyone.

There are other names for the Power of Good, but this is the
one I use. The name "Christ" or "Jesus" brings power that darkness
cannot defeat. Every day when you wake up or whenever you feel
anxious or afraid, you can say this prayer and draw a circle, the
Celtic caim, around yourself, like your Scots and Irish ancestors.
You can remember that courage is fear that has said its prayers. Or,
you can simply say "Jesus" or "God" or "Love" and you won't be
alone. You will have resources for the challenges in front of you.

To encircle yourself with God's love and protection, first, take
a deep breath. Then move slowly in a circle, rotating right to left,
drawing a circle around you with your pointer finger (or finger
next to your thumb). While you rotate yourself slowly say words
like: "I am safe," "God's love surrounds me," "I am in the circle of
God's protection." You will discover that like St. Patrick, you can
do all the right things: wear a mask, wash your hands, practice safe
distancing, be patient with your family, face your fears, and live
with a sense of confidence, knowing you are in the circle of love.

CHAPTER TWO

GRIEF AND FEAR

Where can I go from your spirit?
Or where can I flee from your presence?
If I ascend to heaven, you are there;
if I make my bed in Sheol [the place of darkness and fear],
you are there.
If I take the wings of the morning
and settle at the farthest limits of the sea,
Even there your hand shall lead me,
and your right hand shall hold me fast.
If I say, "Surely the darkness shall cover me,
and the light around me become night,"
even the darkness is not dark to you;
the night is as bright as the day,
for darkness is as light to you. (Psalm 139:7–12, AP)

Courage is fear that has said its prayers. You'll hear me say that throughout this book. It's become a talisman, a source of strength and confidence for me during this time of pandemic. Sometimes courage comes when we pause long enough to see where we are and the resources that are in us and all around us. We discover we are wise and strong enough to face whatever challenges life gives us. Courage also emerges when we discover that within the challenges we face — and the fear that threatens to overcome us — there is a Deep Wisdom and Power that we can trust to guide us to safety. It's everywhere. It's in your heart and soul, and in every act of kindness.

One of my spiritual mentors is African American spiritual guide and magus Howard Thurman, who lived from 1899-1981. He was a boy who grew up to be one of our nation's magi. When he was a boy, not much older than you, growing up in Florida, he went berry picking on a hot summer day. He plunged into the woods behind his home, stuffing berries into his pail and just as many in his mouth. It was a glorious day until he heard a crash of thunder and saw a flash of lightning. He woke up to his surroundings and discovered he had no idea where he was. Filled with panic, he wanted to start running even though he had no idea which path led home. Then he remembered something his grandmother, a wise woman, and another member of the magi, told him, "if you ever are lost, stop, look, listen, and you will eventually see something familiar that will help you find your way."

So, he stopped. He looked to his left and then his right and then ahead and finally behind until he saw something he recognized. He took a few steps, and then there was another flash of lightning and he saw further ahead. And, then another flash and he took a few more steps until he found his way home.

Young Howard realized that the solution was right in front of him if he just paused, breathed deeply, and looked around. The same lightning strikes that frightened him also provided the light that helped him find his way home. He was afraid, but when he stopped to take a deep breath and then look around, he discovered a secret in the storm. The answers you need are found in your fear. The light is hidden in the darkness. Within the storm you will find your direction home.

We hear the word "grief" a lot these days. Everyone, even children, is feeling grief during this time of sickness. Grief is a word we use to describe the loss of anything important to us. We can feel grief when we move to a new town and have to say "goodbye" to friends. We can feel grief when we lose an important soccer or basketball game and don't get the medal we'd hoped for. We can feel grief when we lose a special toy. We can feel grief when we miss people we love and activities that are important to us. Sometimes we wonder when life will get back to normal and we won't feel sad anymore.

Grief is normal and so is fear. It's alright to feel sad right now. I feel sad when I watch the news and see the pain people are feeling. Sometimes tears come to my eyes. I feel sad when I can't go to church or teach a class in person. I feel sad when I need to be on the lookout for people walking by, not feeling comfortable to be too close to people walking on the beach, and not being able to shake hands or hug a friend. I know that you feel sad too!

Fear and grief tell us that our lives are important and that other people matter. They tell us about what we love and what we don't want to live without. These days, people are discovering that their fear and grief reveal what is important in life: family, friends, health, prayer, people who bring our groceries, and people whom we can help. And there is God who often seems hidden, but who is always with us providing a path forward even when we feel alone. Ironically, the other side of grief is celebration and gratitude for all the good things in life, things we would hate to lose.

Most of us are feeling loss these days. We don't like these feelings, but we need to recognize them, and remind ourselves that if we didn't feel this way, we wouldn't be fully alive. That being alive means loving and missing, winning and losing, and succeeding and failing. I believe that even God feels the pain of the world and struggles to give us the wisdom to love one another and work together to cure the Coronavirus.

The Coronavirus pandemic challenges you to be a hero. This may be your first heroic adventure — like Luke Skywalker and Princess Leia, the children from the Chronicles of Narnia, Harry Potter and Hermione Granger, Ulysses, Wonder Woman, Black Panther, or Dr. Strange. They all were afraid when they took the first steps on their adventures and faced powers that seemed greater than themselves. But they discovered a hero within that could be afraid — fear sometimes helps us make good decisions — and not be afraid of being afraid, and not let fear get in the way of greatness.

During this time, we've read books about Ruby Bridges and Rosa Parks. They were afraid but did the right thing. Can you imagine six year old Ruby Bridges going to school with people yelling at her, calling her names, and threatening her just because of the color of her skin? Can you visualize Rosa Parks who wouldn't give up her seat to a white woman, while the bus driver called the police? I bet that they were afraid but they kept their eyes on the prize. They knew that courage is fear that has said its prayers. They learned that love outlasts hate and strength comes from facing your fears and still doing what's right.

You've heard about Martin Luther King, who fought for justice for everyone, most especially the African-American community, the children of slaves who were being treated unjustly in stores, voting, schools, and public parks. He was afraid but God showed him how to become a hero. One evening after a particularly stressful day, Martin Luther King went to bed for the night. On the verge of falling asleep, he received an angry phone call, threatening to harm him and his family. Unable to sleep, King went downstairs to fix a pot of coffee. In the kitchen, he heard the still small voice of God. Here's how King describes what happened that night:

> I was ready to give up. I tried to think of a way to move out of the picture without appearing to be a coward. In this state of exhaustion, when my courage was almost gone, I determined to take my problem to God. My head in my hands, I bowed over the kitchen table and prayed aloud…. "I am here taking a stand for what I believe is right. But now I am afraid. The people are looking to me for leadership, and if I stand before them without strength or courage, they too will falter. I am at the end of my powers. I have nothing left. I've come to the point where I can't face it alone."

Frightened as he was, King heard a voice in the night, a message from God, saying that despite his fear, everything will be alright. King continues his story:

> At that moment I experienced the presence of the divine as I had never experienced him. It seems as though I could hear the quiet assurance of an inner voice, saying, "Stand up for righteousness, stand up for truth, God will be at your side forever.[1]

---

1   Martin Luther King, Jr. *Testament of Hope: The Essential Writings and Speeches of Martin Luther King, Jr.* (edited by James M. Washington), (New York: HarperSanFrancisco, 1986), 509.

King heard God's still small voice of courage and love in the middle of his personal storm. He still felt fear and continued to get threatening calls. He even went to jail for protesting racial injustice, but he could claim that "the outer situation remained the same, but God had given me inner calm."[2]

During this time of global sickness, you learned the twenty-third Psalm with Grandma Kate and me. I read it almost every day to remind us that God is with us regardless of what happens in our lives.

> The Lord is my shepherd, I shall not want.
> He makes me lie down in green pastures;
> he leads me beside still waters;
> he restores my soul.
> He leads me in right paths
> for his name's sake.

> Even though I walk through the darkest valley,
> I fear no evil;
> for you are with me;
> your rod and your staff—
> they comfort me.

> You prepare a table before me
> in the presence of my enemies;
> you anoint my head with oil;
> my cup overflows.
> Surely goodness and mercy shall follow me
> all the days of my life,
> and I shall dwell in the house of God
> my whole life long. (AP)

---

2   Ibid., 509.

Every day during this time of Coronavirus, I repeat this prayerful poem to remind me that even in the dark times God is with me and will provide whatever I need to make it through this and every other crisis I face. It reminds me that I am safe in the storm, and that there is a Power within me that will outlast the virus and every other threat.

Remember, it's alright to be afraid. It's healthy to feel grief and sadness about the things you've lost in this time. Don't hesitate to share your feelings with a trusted adult — your parents or grandparents, spiritual leader, or your church school-teacher or counselor. They care about you and will honor your feelings They will remind you that God loves all of you — your courage and your fear, your anger and your love, and your stress and your peace. God will be with you in the storm and provide a path toward safety.

A SIMPLE PRAYER

The words for today are "energy" and "love." Remember the story of young Howard Thurman. This young Jedi in training (padawan Jedi) found wisdom and courage in the storm by pausing and looking around. You can do the same thing by saying this prayer for just a few minutes every day or when you begin to feel anxious or afraid:

1. Find a comfortable place to sit or stand still.

2. Notice how you feel: your body, emotions, thoughts.

3. Slowly breathe deeply, simply enjoying inhaling.

4. Slowly exhale, simply enjoy letting go.

5. Imagine that breath as the Energy of Life and Love, of God, filling and surrounding you.

6. Do this about ten or twelve times and feel your growing relaxation

Close by silently saying "thank you" to God and the people you love. The storm may not go away immediately. But you will feel a sense of peace and know that on the darkest night, God is your companion.

CHAPTER THREE

LOVE AND KINDNESS

Beloved, let us love one another, because love is from God; everyone who loves is born of God and knows God... for God is love. (1 John 4:7)

People are short tempered and impatient these days. We've been cooped up together in our homes for months. While we hope to get back to normal and are beginning to go back to school and play sports, it's unlikely we'll be going to movies, stadiums, sports arenas, or restaurants for quite awhile. Sports practices and scouting are temporarily resuming but they are carefully organized with proper distancing and masks.

You are wonderful brothers and you love each other. But there are moments when it's just too much companionship. You get on each other's nerves especially when you want to go your own way and play your own games or when you want the other to play with you and he'd rather not. There are moments when you get tired of each other and want to be with someone else, and then there's trouble. Brother trouble — pushing and shoving, sometimes punching and swearing. Parents can feel that way, too. We just need a little space to be by ourselves, get away from it all, and act like everything's normal again.

Now, that sort of friction is normal for brothers and in families. My brother and I often pushed each other around, and as the younger brother I often had to duck for cover. Even sisters get on each other's nerves. But it isn't pretty and deep down you don't like it either. We want to get along, and live in harmony, but even adults are impatient and short tempered with one another these days.

All of us are under stress. I like being at home but being home nearly twenty-four hours each day, especially during the worst months of the virus, can be too much for me too and probably grandma as well. I try to be a saint, and live out my magi spirit, but even saints get upset and raise their voices. That's why going to the beach and closing the door of my study are important to me. They help me get the quiet time I need to breathe deeply, think, write, and enjoy my own company.

A poet who was popular when I was in college, Kahlil Gibran, once counseled, "let there be spaces in your togetherness." That is the type of advice magi or Jedi would give. We all need a little space — some time to ourselves to do just what we want without anyone interrupting us — and that's hard to come by these days. There are times that we need to find space inside our spirits, even if we can't find it outside in our environment.

Now, these days two words have been surfacing in my mind a lot. They are magic words, "kindness" and "love." They are feelings and they are also choices. I believe that we can choose to be kind and we can choose to love especially in difficult times.

Kindness, according to the dictionary means "gentleness," "tenderness," "concern," "care," and "sympathy." It comes from the word "kin," that means "family" or "relative." The word kindness reminds us that we are connected, that we are all in this together, and that our feelings and thoughts matter to one another. We are family, and kindness reminds us to act like a loving family first to one another and then to the rest of the world.

Kindness is a choice. You don't have to like what your brother or parents or grandma or I am doing. But you can still be kind. You can choose to love. You have a choice to take a breath, see the best in your companions, and act with kindness. Boxes often are labeled "handle with care," when there's something fragile inside and that is good advice for our relationships.

Handle with care. Everyone is fragile, everyone can be hurt, everyone carries a burden, and we can choose to treat with compassion and care even when we are stressed out or troubled.

Recently I was teaching on "Ethics in a Time of Pandemic." One of the members mentioned the importance of empathy in making decisions that help other people be treated fairly. Empathy involves feeling the other's feelings. Remembering that others have feelings just like you — feelings of joy, pain, sadness, anger, hurt. Remembering how you feel when someone does something that brings pain or joy to you. Empathy reminds us that everyone, deep down, wants to be loved, respected, appreciated, and heard, just like you do.

Empathy reminds us to practice the Golden Rule, "Do unto others what you would like them to do unto you" or, at least, the Silver Rule, "Do not do to others what you would not like done unto you."

Empathy leads to love. Love is both a feeling and a choice. When you both were born, your parents loved you and your grandparents, Bill and Cathy, and Kate and I loved you. We hadn't gotten to know you but we loved you. It was a feeling of kinship, but also a choice. We have been choosing to love you ever since you were born and we would do anything for you because of our love.

Birds and elephants put their lives at risk to protect their children. It may be instinct but I also believe they are also choosing to love. They are choosing to sacrifice something important — their lives — for something more important, their babies.

Love is a choice. And when we choose love, we are no longer afraid. We know we are connected. We know that love will outlast our fears.

These days, when you watch protests and see signs that say, "Black lives matter," you experience what happens when some people choose not to love. When people hurt others just because of the color of their skin. When people forget that others feel pain and joy and need to be heard, not hurt.

I have a practice that helps me choose to love better. I helps me love people I don't know and even people I don't necessarily like. I say to myself every morning that will "I bless everyone" I meet. To bless means to wish others the best, to see their inner value, to hope that they flourish in terms of what's really important in life, even when I'm not happy with what they are doing. It means to see the goodness — the presence of God — in them and try to bring it out. It also means to love yourself and protect yourself.

Love doesn't mean being a doormat and letting people hurt you! It means caring for others, forgiving them, and trying to find a way to bring happiness to every situation. It means being compassionate with your neighbor and yourself.

For you boys, and for children and youth everywhere, love is a two-way street. Each day you can say to yourself, "I am going to treat my family with love. I am going to speak words of love. When I'm angry, I'm going to share how I feel, honor my own needs, and find a way for all of us to get what we need. I will use my words and hands to love and not to hurt." I can be a love giver, and even when I'm upset, I can make choices that bring out the best in myself and others.

A Simple Prayer.

Each day when you wake up, take a moment to look around and give thanks for being alive. Then, ask yourself, "How can I love the people around me? How can I show my family I love them?" Think of ways you can add to their happiness. Then make a choice to love even when it's tough.

During the day, you may become impatient and tempted to strike out physically or verbally. At that moment, pause and remember your commitment to love. Take a breath. This is the time to breathe deeply before you say something or lash out.

You are getting mature enough to choose love. To see the best in yourself and see the best in the ones around you. Choose love and behaviors that express how you feel, your joy and pain, that add to the love in your family and the world.

CHAPTER FOUR

HOPE

"Hope" is the thing with feathers –
That perches in the soul –
And sings the tune without the words –
And never stops — at all — (Emily Dickinson)[3]

Now faith is the assurance of things hoped for, the conviction of
things not seen. (Hebrews 11:1)

Going to sleep can be difficult. There are times you don't want
to sleep alone. There are times when you wake up in the middle
of the night and run downstairs to your parents' or grandparents'
room. Or you can't sleep and wait for daylight to come when it's
ok to get up and play.

Most nights I go to bed thinking about tomorrow, thinking
about what will come, both expected and unexpected, with the
new day. I review the day that is ending and give thanks for good
things I've experienced. There are lots of good things, aren't there?
Birthday parades with fire engines, police cars, and friends passing
by at a safe distance. Action figures and Lego toys. Playing soccer,
basketball, and baseball. Cuddling with your parents and grandparents. Imagination. Henry Danger and Thor, the Avengers and
Star Wars. Reading and art. Home. Family. I think about those
things and then I pray to wake up tomorrow to something special,
something simple that has never happened before, some of the same
old but the same old with a new spirit.

---

3   Emily Dickenson, *The Complete Poems* (New York: Little, Brown and
     Company, 1976), 116.

Each morning I wake up with the words from the Bible, "this is the day that God has made and I will rejoice and be glad it in." This is one of my spiritual anchors and a guidepost for every magus. It's my way of saying that even though I can't go everywhere I want these days and I have to do a lot of things differently than I used to, and I have to be more careful than I want to be, I am alive and today is filled with possibility. I'll make mistakes and miss some good things in the course of the day. But, and it is the great "but," I will have the opportunity to do things I've never done before, think new thoughts, write new words, read new words or old words, like the Hardy Boys mysteries I read first sixty years ago, then thirty years ago with your Dad, and now I'm reading with you.

Hope is the dream of tomorrow. Hope is the open future. The possibility of something new happening, of making different choices, and creating something from your imagination. Hope is the Great Work that you and no one else can do. Hope recognizes that small as you think you are you can make a difference. You can change the world.

I hope a lot these days. I hope the pandemic will be over soon. I hope that we can have a vaccine or cure in 2021. I hope I can drive you to school and pick you up after school soon. I hope I can get an ice-cream with you at Four Seas or Polar Zone or Gone Chocolate. I hope we can get Pizza at Crisp and burgers at Five Guys, and someday eat inside again. I hope to watch you play soccer and basketball with your team. I hope that everyone in our nation will be treated equally and that we will protect our planet for future generations of humans and non-humans. Hope is the future that may come if we keep the faith, and do the right things like wearing a mask, washing our hands, and keeping safe distancing. Hope is the trust that we can make different choices and use our freedom to create not destroy, and love and not hate.

Hope is the dream of tomorrow. That the world can be different. That we can be different. That we will grow and have the freedom to do someone only we can do with our unique and awesome lives. Real hope leads to real action to change the world.

You are just getting started, boys. In many ways, you are all hope. And so are all the children of the United States and the world. You are learning a multitude of ways you can grow up. Hope is imagining what you can become. The future in your eyes and in your heart. The future in your imagination. And so, we, as parents and grandparents, teachers, and magi, tend to your hopes. Keeping our own hopes alive though we have already traveled far and have made choices that have determined much of our future. But in being with you, we discover new futures and we hope for the good things that may come if we do our part.

Hope is imagination but it is also action. We need to hope big and think big. I hope that after the pandemic, we will treat each other better — that skin color won't be the source of pain and hurt. That we will take better care of the Earth. That we will remember what is important and not get stuck in the small details. That we will have leaders who care for others and put the planet ahead of popularity. And I hope that every child has enough to eat, schools, and loving homes. God can't build our hopes for us without our partnership. God can give us a dream, but we have to use our arms, legs, hands, and heart to make it come true.

A wise teacher, Abraham Joshua Heschel, a member of the magi, once recalled after marching for peace with Martin Luther King, "I felt like my legs were praying." Another wise teacher Teresa of Avila said you are God's arms and feet. Right now, if we want change, we need to remember that we are the ones we have been waiting for, as poet June Jordan affirmed. Without us, God's dream for the world won't come true. Whether older or younger, we are the seeds of the future we hope for, the dream of a new day, the promise of beauty to come.

So, go ahead. Have high hopes. Practice for the adventures ahead. You will have plenty of adventures in the year to come. But always hope for love. For family. For justice. For those who can't speak for themselves. For what the new day will bring.

A Simple Prayer

Take time as usual to pause and be still a few minutes. Take some deep breaths. Just relaxing and letting go of any stress you might be feeling. While you're quietly relaxing, think about your hopes for the future. What things will give you joy once you're able to go out and play, go back to school, and see friends, without having to worry about masks and safe distancing? What things will give your parents and loved ones joy? Do you have a hope for the world? How do you want the world to be different for everyone? Think about these things. Then take a moment to pray for the future or visualize the world to come as you say, perhaps, "God help me and every creature find happiness. Help me do something to build a better future today."

Hope is a bit like constructing a Lego building. You have an idea about what you're doing and then step by step you put things together. Think about what you want to see in your life and the world, and then ask for wisdom — and kids have wisdom — to achieve this by simple acts today. You can begin changing your world today one action at a time.

CHAPTER FIVE

TRUST

> When you pass through the waters, I will be with you;
> and through the rivers, they shall not drown you;
> when you walk through fire you shall not be burned,
> and the flame shall not harm you. (Isaiah 43:2, my paraphrase)

Long ago before astronomers explained meteors and comets, the people of a small village observed what they thought were stars falling to earth. They ran back and forth in the village, filled with fear and saying to one another, "the sky is falling, the sky is falling, we're doomed." To them the shooting stars meant the end of the world. As they ran fearfully through the village, knocking on every door, they finally came to the home of the wise woman and wise man of the village. When they shared their fears, the wise ones gazed thoughtfully at the sky, and then responded, "Yes, the stars are falling, but look at the stars that stay in place!"

Trust matters most when the sky is falling. Life is a process of constant change. Sometimes change makes us feel like our world has turned upside down. You have changed radically from the time you were a fertilized egg no larger than the head of a pin to a little baby totally dependent on your mother's care and now to a living, breathing, playing, loving persons you are today. Over the past few months, you have had to adapt to unforeseen changes and grow up faster than you anticipated. And there are lots of changes ahead. The world is changing, more than we can imagine over the last several months. Everything has been turned upside down. The familiar has become the unusual. What we depended on, taking for granted without thinking about it, has become exceptional. This likely will be the case for years to come even after vaccines are available to everyone.

Life is always changing and unpredictable. But, as the wise ones of the village noted there are a few things we can count on, and that's where trust comes in. Trust is the belief that there are persons and things we can depend on despite all the changes we experience.

Trust is based on dependability. We need to count on others to support us in good times and bad, regardless of inconvenience. Trust means keeping your word and your commitments. If you say you're going to do something, you follow through. If you are a friend or parent or brother or sister, you support one another even when it's not convenient or you need to make a sacrifice. That's the person I try to be for you.

Trust depends on truthfulness. That's why we counsel you to tell the truth even if it may cost you something. Most of the time truth-telling is good for everyone involved. When you make a mistake, let people you trust know about it. If you tell the truth with small things, you will be trusted with large things.

There are times, when you may need to keep silence or not reveal what you know to protect others or yourself, but these moments are exceptional. Tell the truth about yourself and tell the truth about others. Pay attention to facts, and make sure that when you speak about others, you know what happened before you say something. You can ruin another person's reputation or your own by a few poorly chosen and inaccurate words.

These days, when national leaders purposely lie or challenge established scientific facts to increase their popularity, our ability to trust them diminishes and we are confused about the right course of action. As a wise person once said, you are entitled to your own opinions but you are not entitled to your own facts. Be a person as good as your word, and as honest as the truth you tell.

The greatest trust involves trust that the universe is good and that universe supports goodness and beauty. Trust in small things is connected to trusting the big things in life. To trust the future means following another wise one Theodore Parker who said that in spite of all of our problems, the moral arc of history bends toward justice. For us, this means to trust in God so that in all the storms of life, we know that we are protected, that God is with us, and will not abandon us.

These days, the world isn't always trustworthy. We are concerned that others might carry the Coronavirus. We prepare to keep our loved ones and ourselves safe from the virus, even though in the past our nation's leadership couldn't always be counted on to tell us the truth. But we can trust those who truly love us, who tell us the truth in ways we can understand, and who stand by us in the darkest night and brightest day. And we can become persons known by our honesty and faithfulness, who keep our word and stand by our friends and family.

A Simple Prayer

Imagine yourself in a storm at sea, with waves tossing your boat around. Feel your uncertainty and fear as the waves and wind buffet your boat like a small toy. Then imagine that Jesus is with you. Visualize what Jesus looks like, his words to you, and his presence. How do you feel with Jesus beside you? What is it like to have him in the boat with you?

Think of persons who you would trust to help you in a storm. Who are they? What characteristics make them trustworthy? Imagine them with Jesus in the boat with you.

Now, think of how you can help people who are in trouble. What characteristics do you need to develop to be trusted by others?

You are never alone. In the storms around us, whether at sea or in this time of sickness, you are safe. God is with you, and you are loved by God and your parents and grandparents.

CHAPTER SIX

JOY

This is the day that God has made, let us rejoice and be
glad in it. (Psalm 118:24)

As you know, magi constantly study. You can't know too much
about God, the universe, science, health, and practices that change
our lives and the world. Magi believe that our goal in life, regardless
of who we are and the nature of our gifts, is to become as much
like God as possible, to be synch with the Wise Creativity of the
Universe, the order of the heavens above, and the creative Spirit
within, and then share that order and beauty with the world.

Magi often use chants or runes to align ourselves with the
inner and outer Wisdom and to take our role in confronting the
powers of destruction and healing the earth. These chants give us
power and courage and the wisdom to respond to the problems
we face.

Many of my chants and affirmations come from the Bible, a
book revealing the Wisdom of the Universe in stories describing
the adventures of persons and nations. Every morning I say the
words to provide guidance and energy for the day ahead, "This is
the day that God has made and I will rejoice and be glad in it." I am
repeating these words to you because they are one of my personal
anchors and are essential for any magi's spiritual tool kit. Notice
the word rejoice, or "have joy." Joy is an attitude toward life, a
sense that life is good and beautiful despite the challenges we face.
Joy involves the ability to see the moral and spiritual arc of history
moving through the world and your life and believing that love
and goodness are at work and will eventually triumph in the world.

Joy is a sense of blessedness at the simple wonder of being alive
and the deep truth that we are part of an adventure much larger
than ourselves, an unending story of evolving Spirit and Love. In

the middle of challenges that they face, you can see the joy in Yoda, Obi Wan Kenobi, Dumbledore or Gandalf, that is absent in Darth Vader, Gollum, and Voldemort.

The forces of destruction are powerful but they have no joy. They don't laugh or smile, or delight in simple things. They can't love. They can't make fun of themselves or enjoy other's humorous comments about them. You can see a joy amid the struggle in Luke Skywalker, Harry Potter, and Hermione Granger that is lacking in those who try to undermine their missions.

Joy is a spiritual state. Joy is a choice as well as a blessing. As a wise person, Viktor Frankl, who spent many years unjustly held in prison in World War II, counsels, they can take everything away from a person except their freedom to choose their attitude toward life, their ability to choose their way.

So, each morning I proclaim my spiritual anchor, "This is the day that God has made and I will rejoice and be glad in it." This becomes the enchanted looking glass through which I see the world even on difficult days. This chant becomes the spiritual gyroscope that gets me back to balance when I become upset. In saying it, I see the world differently. The challenges of life won't go away and life is often difficult but there is a Deeper Reality that is present even in the most difficult times and that Reality cannot be defeated by destruction, darkness, or virus.

Joy inspires you to be a happy and peaceful warrior. The fight is on, and the battle is hard, but there is joy in the journey. Joy is spiritual Kung Fu, reminding you that you can keep your head when others are panicking and that you have the ability to choose peace of mind and happiness despite what's going on around you. The joy of affirming that life is good and you are always guided by a Wisdom and Power greater than yourself. The joy of knowing that goodness and love — the moral and spiritual arcs of history — will triumph despite this present darkness. Long after disease and destruction, and people who promote disease and destruction, are off the scene, joy will endure. Love and joy last forever.

A Simple Prayer

Begin each day with the words "This is the day that God has made, and I will rejoice and be glad in it." Repeat them slowly a few times, thinking about what they mean. Breathe deeply, creativity and wisdom flowing through you. Feel energy and love filling with each breath. Look for beauty and goodness everywhere and commit yourself to bringing beauty and love out of its hiding place. Give thanks for the goodness and beauty you see in the world.

There is plenty of trouble out there. The world needs "super-heroes" like you. Fight evil with a smile and kindness, but if you must challenge the forces of evil with body and soul, be guided by a horizon of hope that the evil won't last forever and that there is good even in Darth Vader, and that your goal is peace and not destruction. Stand with the forgotten and bullied, trusting that God's arc of goodness will triumph in the end.

CHAPTER SEVEN

CREATIVITY

I am about to do a new thing;
now it springs forth, do you not perceive it?
I will make a way in the wilderness.
and rivers in the desert. (Isaiah 43:19)

Children are creative by nature. Children are imaginative by nature. I know that you are creative, imagining alternative universes, becoming superheroes fighting epoch battles, and seeing yourself make game-winning baskets or touchdowns. When we are children, we live life out loud, imagining ourselves to be superheroes, star athletes, knights and Jedi, private detectives, and princesses. We are intended to think big, have big ideas, and then put them into practice. Sadly, many adults surrender their creativity, worried about making a mistake or standing out in the crowd as different.

You are creative and imaginative by nature, and you can live out loud, seeing yourself as superhero or world shaper, love giver and light giver.

One of my favorite Bible verses describes Jesus as growing in wisdom and stature. At twelve years of age, in the Jerusalem Temple, Jesus committed himself to a life of learning and growth (Luke 2:41–52). Jesus committed himself to love and hospitality every day of his life. Jesus saw himself as a work in progress recognizing that there is always more to learn, do, create, and love. God's world is always more than we can imagine and God always has something new to show us.

We are created to be creators. Each of us is unique in terms of our experience and behavior. No one experiences the world from our perspective and each moment is an opportunity for you to make a unique and creative response to the world around us.

I have always created with ideas and words. To quote the philosopher Alfred North Whitehead, my whole life has been an adventure of ideas. When I was a child, I invented baseball and football leagues and was a star player. I imagined myself making the final putt to win the Masters or the British Open. I created whole countries with governments and big cities. I drew maps of towns and designed houses. Later in life, after reading the *Lord of the Rings*, I imagined myself as Gandalf the Great and even had a staff that I carried with me when I walked in the woods. As a college student, I visualized myself as a professor and then became one and then saw myself as an author and then started writing. When I became a grandparent, I discovered a patch of grass and a stream in the shadow of our high rise in Washington DC that I renamed the One Aker Wood, where Jack and I could imagine ourselves having adventures with Pooh, Piglet, Eeyore, Owl, Kanga and Roo, Rabbit, and Christopher Robin. I even wrote some books about it! These days I delight when you (the youngest grandchild) wield Thor's hammer to confront the powers of chaos and destruction. I rejoice when the two of us (the oldest grandchild) face off in the NBA Finals and you make a three point shot to win the championship.

During the Spring and Summer of 2020, we were sheltering in place. We stayed home and don't see a lot of people. We did what is right in this time of pandemic — we practiced safe physical distancing and wore masks. But that didn't keep you from creating. And you will keep creating long after you return to school.

To be a magus is to be creative, to look at the heavens, and then bring cosmic order and creativity to earth. To be a scientist and mathematician is to be a creator, to imagine theories of the universe or numbers and then see if you are right. To be an athlete like Michael Jordan, Larry Bird, Serena Williams, or Lionel Messi — they play basketball, tennis, and soccer, but create new ways of playing the game. Think of the wondrous creativity of the books and movies you read and then look behind them to J.K. Rowling, Stan Lee, J.R.R. Tolkien, C.S. Lewis, and Madeleine L'Engle. They were all children once, and they remained childlike in spirit. They all had vivid imaginations and then took a chance on sharing their creativity with the world.

You are a creator. You bring something new into the world. Think big and then think bigger. Don't let others place a limit on your dreams. Don't let COVID stifle your imagination. Let the concrete problems you daily face at home, school, and the world become the birthplace of new possibilities. Each moment is new and wonderful, and you are making it happen by your hopes, dreams, and creativity.

A Simple Prayer

Relax and let your imagination run free without limitations. What do you enjoy doing? What things are you really good at? Imagine your greatness in these areas. Imagine making a difference. Imagine making a difference by doing what you love. Remember the words of Eric Liddell from the movie, "Chariots of Fire." He was an Olympic runner, known for his unusual running style. He won a Gold Medal in the 1924 Paris Olympics. He told his sister, who asked why he was so committed to running, "God made me fast and when I run I can feel God's pleasure."

Do something joyful today. Move your mind and feet and hands. Feel God's pleasure when you run, jump, imagine, and create, and life will be good even in difficult times. You will bring beauty and joy to the world.

CHAPTER EIGHT

PLAYFULNESS

> When God established the heavens, I [Sophia, God's wise com-
> panion] was there joyfully creating,
> when God drew a circle on the face of the ocean.
> when God made the skies above,
> when God established the fountains of the ponds and streams,
> when God separated sea from land,
> so that the earth would not be flooded,
> when God marked out the earth beneath us,
> then I was beside God, like a little child playing,
> and I was daily God's delight,
> rejoicing before God always,
> rejoicing in God's inhabited world
> and delighting in the human race. (Psalm 8:27–31, my para-
> phrase)

Some adults say, "it's never too late to have a happy childhood."
A friend of mine has a license plate on her sporty convertible
that reads, "How Fun." Yes, we all need some fun and time
to play, and the opportunity to do things for no other reason than
the pure joy of it.

Well, boys, this is your childhood and you are living it out in a
time of national crisis. I often worry about this time as "lost time"
in your childhood and that with the Coronavirus, the masks, the
physical distancing, you will lose some of the innocence and pure
joy of childhood. You have lamented not being able to see friends,
go to school, and play on sports teams. It's hard to go to the beach
without when you have to worry about getting too close to other
people, none of whom have masks. No child should have to worry
about such things. And, on Memorial Day, May 25, 2020, you
asked questions about an African American man who was killed
by a police officer in Minnesota and now you are asking about the

peaceful protests that are occurring across the United States. You were worried because some of our friends were marching in the peaceful protests. But you responded by making a "Black Lives Matter" poster that we hang on our front door.

You boys have been fortunate because you have had a childhood! You have time and place to play, let your mind roam, and explore new ideas. Some kids live in poverty or have lost their homes due to war or natural disasters and they have had to grow up quickly. Still, every child deserves a happy childhood, living out their unique dreams, imagining alternative worlds, pretending to be superheroes, playing safely with friends, and living in a home with good food, good water, a bed to sleep on, and loving adults. It's the job of our nation's leaders and older people like your parents and grandparents to make sure every child can enjoy their childhood.

When I was your age, almost sixty years ago, times were different than today. We didn't have cell phones, computers, cable television, and parents didn't worry about our safety. When I was nine or ten, my buddy Richard Jenkins and I used to ride our bikes all over town, play cowboys and Indians along the Salinas River, go horseback riding without adults to guide us, and walk to our sports practices and scouts. Mom would say, "Be careful and be back by dinner," when we went out after lunch.

Your world is good today. It is filled with great beauty. And also worry. We need to keep our eyes on you more than my parents did, but you still have time and space to play. I give thanks for that every day and Kate's and my role in nurturing your lives.

I like to play although my play is different than most folks. In many ways, magi are champions at "high play." They march to the beat of a different drummer. I don't play quidditch like Harry Potter and the wizards of Hogwarts, I seldom play golf or ski, though I play a slow game of basketball and football with you and can still hit a baseball a long way. I play with ideas just like I played baseball and cowboys and Indians when I was a child. I play on the beach, watching the sunrise and clouds every morning. I play with words and try to write a thousand every morning! I play when I pray and meditate. And I play with you. I am glad you have invited me into the world of Harry Potter (as Dumbledore), the Avengers, and basketball games. Though I am closer to seventy than ten, I still can have a happy childhood — and an imaginative and energetic adulthood — every day, in part because of you.

Can you imagine God playing? That's what the bible verses at the beginning of this chapter say! God playfully brings forth galaxies, planets, pangolins and ostriches, right whales and anteaters, flamingos and human beings. Can you imagine God's joy at your creativity and imagination? Can you imagine God playing along with you, urging you to do something that might even surprise God?

Wise people say angels can fly because they take themselves lightly! Playfulness is about taking yourself lightly. About recognizing that there is a humorous side to your most serious tasks. When I play professor and wear my black robe with a hood like the wizards and a Tam O' Shanter, like Dumbledore, I look pretty funny lined up with all the other professors. When I put on my white robe with my stole, or tallit or prayer shawl, for church services I look strange too. I play at praying and preaching. All I need is a magician's hat to complete the picture!

Humor keeps us from feeling so important that we see ourselves as different from other people. I don't trust a priest or politician who doesn't laugh or cry or can't make fun of themselves. Life is too serious not to laugh.

Playfulness is about letting your imagination be free. A child's imagination gives birth to an adult's creativity. A child's play gives birth to an inventor's ingenuity and an author's inspiration.

These are hard times. But you can still play. You can still delight in wrestling with our Golden Doodle Tucker. You can explore universes in your mind. You can tell jokes and watch humorous home videos on television. You can shoot a basket, kick a soccer ball, and play corn hole. You can be a child, letting us adults worry about the challenges of living in this time of pandemic and protest.

A Simple Prayer

Today, just simply give thanks for the chance to play. Think of all the things that make it possible for you to play — home, family, toys, and so on. And, then say "thank you" to your loved ones and to a world and its Playful Creator who makes a world where you can have fun, play, and do new things. And, then go out — or in — and play! Run and jump, stretch your muscles and imagination, and live your dreams. God is playing beside you!

CHAPTER NINE

ADVENTURE

> Now GOD said to Abram, "Go from your country and
> your kindred and your father's house to the land that I will
> show you. (Genesis 12:1)

Yesterday, after our time of homeschooling, we watched the
"Lord of the Rings: The Desolation of Smaug," a film that describes
the adventures of the Hobbit Bilbo and a band of dwarves, led by
Thorin. These days, life is adventurous even though we aren't leav-
ing our homes. Some pilgrims chart undiscovered territory. Other
adventurers go on journeys without distance. They can range the
whole universe from an observatory or change the world from a
jail cell. Our adventures may take us off course, but in losing our
way, we may discover new horizons of possibility. As J.R.R. Tolkien
says in *The Fellowship of the Rings*, "not all who wander are lost."

Every adventure involves both risk and opportunity. God told
Abraham and Sarah to go to a new land and start a new life. They
were nervous and knew they would miss their friends but they
visualized a new land on the horizon and then embarked on an
adventure into the unknown.

To embrace the unfamiliar and novel we may need to temporarily or permanently give up the familiar and habitual. We need
to try new things. We need to let go of what no longer works. We
may need to recognize that it is not where we started from or where
we planned to go that is important, but where our voyage takes us
and what happens on the way.

Mapmakers in Europe before the time of Columbus inscribed
the words "there is no more," or *ne plus ultra*, at the edges of their
maps. They assumed that there was nothing beyond the horizon.
They were unaware of the bounties of the unknown land which
we call home. After the explorations of Columbus and others,

they revised their maps with the words, "there is more," or *plus ultra*, to indicate the wonders of the far horizon. While they were unaware of the Rocky Mountains and the Mississippi River and the California coastline, and while they couldn't fully imagine the First American inhabitants, they now realized that what we know is always incomplete. The imaginative arc of history lures us toward new horizons. They made lots of mistakes especially in actions that destroyed our nation's First Inhabitants. They also went on great adventures.

Plus Ultra

There is always more waiting for us somewhere over the rainbow. Thousands of years earlier, I suspect that other great explorers, the parents of the First Americans, looking across the Bering Sea at what is now known as Alaska also exclaimed "there is more" and then crossed into their new-found land as our continent's first human inhabitants.

There is no end to the adventures that lie before us, both big and small. First, there is the adventure of every new day. Each day is a holy adventure, unlike any before. What new thing will happen today? What new possibility will emerge because you woke up today? Those who look for adventures will surely have them.

Our adventures these days are both cosmic and microscopic. They are cosmic as we gaze at the starry sky and imagine a fourteen-billion-year, trillion-galaxy universe. How small we seem on a starry Cape Cod night! Our adventures are also microscopic as scientists in laboratories seek a vaccine and cure for the invisible Coronavirus. We don't know their names, but they will save millions of lives. Heroes and adventurers are often incognito, unknown, and yet they change the world. We can be amazed at our circulatory, nervous, immune, and digestive systems, and the millions of operations must occur for us to see, walk, talk, or write.

The Coronavirus will not put an end to our adventures. We can be adventurous despite what's happening around us. Young

Anne Frank describes what it means to grow up from the confines of an attic during the Nazi pandemic. Nelson Mandela spent three decades as a political prisoner on Robben Island, his soul free as a bird. After he was released, he was willing to seek reconciliation with the South African whites who imprisoned him. Martin Luther King writes the "Letter from the Birmingham Jail," reminding people of faith that to love God you need to make a commitment to justice. Their bodies were confined but their spirits soared.

For adventurers, this can be the time of your life. No day is a lost day. Each day can be a heroic journey as you train to be a magus, Jedi, or justice seeker. Venture forth, my laddies! Create new worlds, lasses!

A Simple Prayer

Remember Dr. Seuss' book, *All the Places You'll Go*. He describes the adventures that can happen to any child as the years unfold. Life begins with a dream and then harvests adventures. What adventures await you today? What new thing do you want to do today? What activity will help you grow larger in spirit and ability? What's frightening, but — if you do it — will bring joy to your heart and a sense that you are stronger, braver, and more creative than you imagine. Ask God for adventures and you will receive them. See today as the opportunity to push your limits, do something new, and create something that's never existed before.

Chapter Ten

Peace

Jesus stood among his frightened followers and said, "Peace be with you." (John 20:19)

This pandemic has changed our world in ways we could not have imagined in March 2020. Sadly, the Coronavirus is not the only tragedy we face these days. Remember when we viewed a video of an African American man, George Floyd, who died in police custody. When he woke up on Monday, May 25, George Floyd never expected to die. He never expected to be the victim of police brutality. You saw the videos and you had a lot of questions. What we saw was frightening and there is no way to justify such violence, especially when it is committed by those whose job is to serve and protect.

We responded to your questions about his death and racism, and hatred based on the differences in color and culture. Trying to make sense of what is impossible to explain. Hate, violence, and prejudice. Black people angry and afraid, and white people angry and afraid. We reassured you that you were safe and reminded you that you need to be on the side of those who experience injustice. You need to stand by those who are in pain and forgotten. You need to delight in all the colors of the rainbow and learn that every color has a beauty of its own.

During the Coronavirus pandemics, we hear people say that "we're all in this together." That wasn't the case for George Floyd or Breonna Taylor nor is it the case for many people of color who experience violence and injustice every day. When we say, "we're all in this together," we affirm that Black Lives Matter. Every life matters and deserves to be treated with respect and compassion. "We're all in this together" also means that we need to care for those who are forgotten and vulnerable and treated unjustly in our community, and that includes folks we've talked about in church — persons who are homeless, children who can't afford school lunches or backpacks and school supplies, children separated from their parents at our nation's borderlands, and persons of color who are often mistreated just because of the color of their skin. Black lives matter! Immigrant children's lives matter! Poor people's lives matter! Blue lives matter! First American lives matter! Right whale lives matter! When we say "all lives matter," we mean everyone but most especially the hurt and forgotten.

There is a battle out there — the battle of Coronavirus, poverty, violence, and racism, and we need to feel peace, and we need to be peacemakers. We need to be peaceful warriors, changing the world without hate. Using the most powerful force in the world — Love. We need to follow the better angels of our nature, as Abraham Lincoln said. Lincoln knew that even in war, we need to claim our role as agents of the moral arc of history. We need to seek peace even when we protect what is most important to us.

As a member of the magi, I know that peace begins in our hearts and words and homes. Think peace. Watch what you think about. Root out, like Grandma Kate in her garden, thoughts of hate, thoughts that separate the world into us and them, and good guys and bad guys. As Luke Skywalker discovers, there is good in Darth Vader, and when we see it, we may help the other person feel it too. Speak peace. Words are important. They can heal or hurt.

Always do your best to speak words of peace. You can share how you feel without hurting someone else or judging someone else. Speak in "I statements" — "I don't like what you're doing," "I would like to play with that now," "I'm upset by what you did." Sometimes peace means being still, taking a few deep breaths, and holding your tongue when it will add to the confusion or conflict in a situation. Other times, it means standing up against a bully or doing what's right even if it's not popular, and still seeing the goodness in those whose behavior or attitudes bother you. Everyone carries a burden these days, and peace means acting with kindness. Looking for the best in those around you and listening to their feelings.

Peace may mean protesting injustice and not letting bullies get their way. You can be a peaceful and happy warrior. You can protest and pray all at the same time! That's what you learn in martial arts like Kung Fu or Aikido. You can be strong and not use your strength to hurt another person, even though you can. Remember when I taught you Reiki healing touch. I told you that from now on, you are to use your hands to heal and not hurt. That's the way of peace: to be part of the energy of love and bring love to every situation.

Peace means looking at the big picture. Peace of mind comes from knowing you are part of something bigger than yourself. You are part of the universe, a child of the galaxies, and stars. You are part of this planet and its seasons. You are part of a world of plants and animals and you are part of the human race. You are part of the great moral arc, God in the world, and the moral arc aims at justice and peace. Though you are small, and all of us are, we can think big and bring peace right where we are. Our hearts can be as large as the Milky Way galaxy. Our imaginations can crisscross the skies. We can love deeply and fully and bring beauty to the world. We can, as another sage said, do something beautiful for God.

The world finds peace one action at a time, one moment at a time, one person at a time. Let there be peace on earth and let it begin with you.

A Simple Prayer

Make a commitment today to be a peacemaker. Bring peace to every encounter. Speak words of peace. Share love. Ask God to give you peace and patience. Ask God to give you the right words and right acts to bring peace on earth and goodwill for all. Pray for people you don't like and learn to see the good in them and bring it out by your words and deeds.

When you're angry, breathe deeply. Be still, and then ask for guidance as to the words and acts that will be best for you and those around you.

Be strong, be brave, but always be kind. Let peace begin with you. The future depends on it!

CHAPTER ELEVEN

IN THE END, LOVE

> And now faith, hope, and love abide, these three; and the greatest of these is love. (I Corinthians 13:13)

This book was a labor of love, and my love for you never ends. It was also a labor of love for other children and their parents, significant others, and grandparents. As your grandfather, as long as I have breath, I will continue to share my wisdom, give you counsel, protect you from ill, and most of all love you. You were born in love. Love has guided your path. Love is your destination. COVID-19 will eventually pass, but love will last forever.

So, above all, love. Let love be your inspiration and goal. Love for the world. Love for people who struggle, love for outsiders, love for those who are bullied and picked on, even love for bullies, and love for this good earth. Love for right whales and pangolins. Love for God and everything God creates. Be God's love in the world. Love lasts forever.

ALSO BY BRUCE EPPERLY

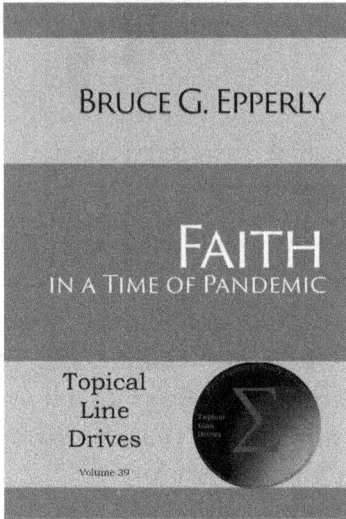

How can we respond spiritually when a pandemic hits our nation? How can our faith help us to face our fears, going beyond panic and denial, to hopeful and courageous action?

$5.99 Paperback
$2.99 eBook

Our lives have been disrupted by a pandemic, but at some point we will find a new normal. What will we do then? Better, what should we do then?

$9.99 Paperback
$4.99 eBook

www.ingramcontent.com/pod-product-compliance
Lightning Source LLC
Chambersburg PA
CBHW031616040426

42452CB00006B/549